I am Just as Special:

How to be a Sibling of a Special Needs Child

Written by Lena Hanna

Illustrated by Daniel Naranjo

Copyright © 2021 Lena Hanna

ISBN: 978-1-7364988-3-5 (Paperback)
ISBN: 978-1-7364988-4-2 (Ebook)
ISBN: 978-1-7364988-8-0 (Hardcover)

All rights reserved. No part of this publication may be reproduced, distributed, or transmitted in any form or by any means, including photocopying, recording, or other electronic or mechanical methods, without the prior written permission of the publisher, except in the case of brief quotations embodied in critical reviews and certain other noncommercial uses permitted by copyright law.

To my dearest Olivia,

Thank you for being you. You have such a huge heart, and you make me so proud.

Love Always,
Mommy

My name is Olivia, and I am four.
Let me tell you what it was like before.
I did not have brothers or sisters, you see.
It used to be only my Mommy and me.

I grew up with love, we were as close as could be.
I was special to her; she was special to me.
I knew I was cherished by my Mommy each day.
I was her most special princess in every way.

Then one day, my mom broke the news and said there would soon be another.
"We are having a baby boy – you are going to have a brother!"

"Noooo!" was the only thing that I could scream. "A brother?! I hope this is a bad dream."

"Olivia, my princess, you'll love one another.
You two will be best friends as sister and brother!"

But I was afraid of the things that would change.
A baby would certainly make our home strange!
A baby would whimper. A baby would cry.
I liked that it was just my Mommy and I!

Her tummy grew bigger, but something was wrong.
I saw Mommy cry, though she tried to stay strong.

She told me my brother had a broken heart.
"At first, we will have to spend time far apart."
She told me a surgery was what he would need.
His health would be fragile and not guaranteed.

Soon the day came when my brother was born.
His heart had some problems, like Mom had warned.
I wasn't allowed to meet him that first day.
I hoped and prayed that he would be okay.

Soon he was released,
and he finally got to come home.
I got to meet him. Now I had a brother of my own.
I felt a lot of feelings, I was happy and excited.
But I was also nervous, and I felt a little frightened.

The first time I saw him, his skin looked quite blue.
My Mommy said that's something broken hearts do.
"He might even get a bit worse for a while.
But doctors will help him," she said with a smile.

My family had changed. Yes, that I could see.
I hoped very much it would still include me.

My mom did not have as much time as before.
We played less together, which scared me much more.

My brother got every last speck of attention.
I understood why, but it filled me with tension.
I used to feel happy and smile quite a lot.
I used to feel special, and then I did not.

After about five weeks, came surgery day.
I waved to my parents as they drove away.
Alone with my brother was where they would stay.
I missed them a lot and did not feel okay.

It seemed like forever, but then they came home.
And, somehow, I continued feeling alone.
I cried when I felt like I could not be strong.
I wondered if it was my fault things went wrong.

I wanted things back to the way they had been,
But even back home it was all about him!
What could I do now? What could do the trick?
Maybe to be loved, I had to be sick.

I thought maybe nobody could hear my cries.
But one day, my Mommy prepared a surprise!
A girls' day together at the Princess Place.
Like old times, I had a huge grin on my face!
"I've missed spending time with you," Mommy then said.
"You're special to me, you're my daughter and friend."
As Mommy kept talking, I danced and I twirled.
"You're my favorite princess in the whole world!"

Soon, my baby brother began to grow strong.
With us all together, I know I belong.
My family's perfect the way that we are.
Even if sometimes there are things that get hard.

I got used to having my brother around.
He cracks up and giggles at my silly sounds!
I play games with him, and we play with his toys.
His face lights up and he makes a cute cooing noise!

I feel so big when I help out – and I am!
My mom needs the help, and I'm glad that I can!

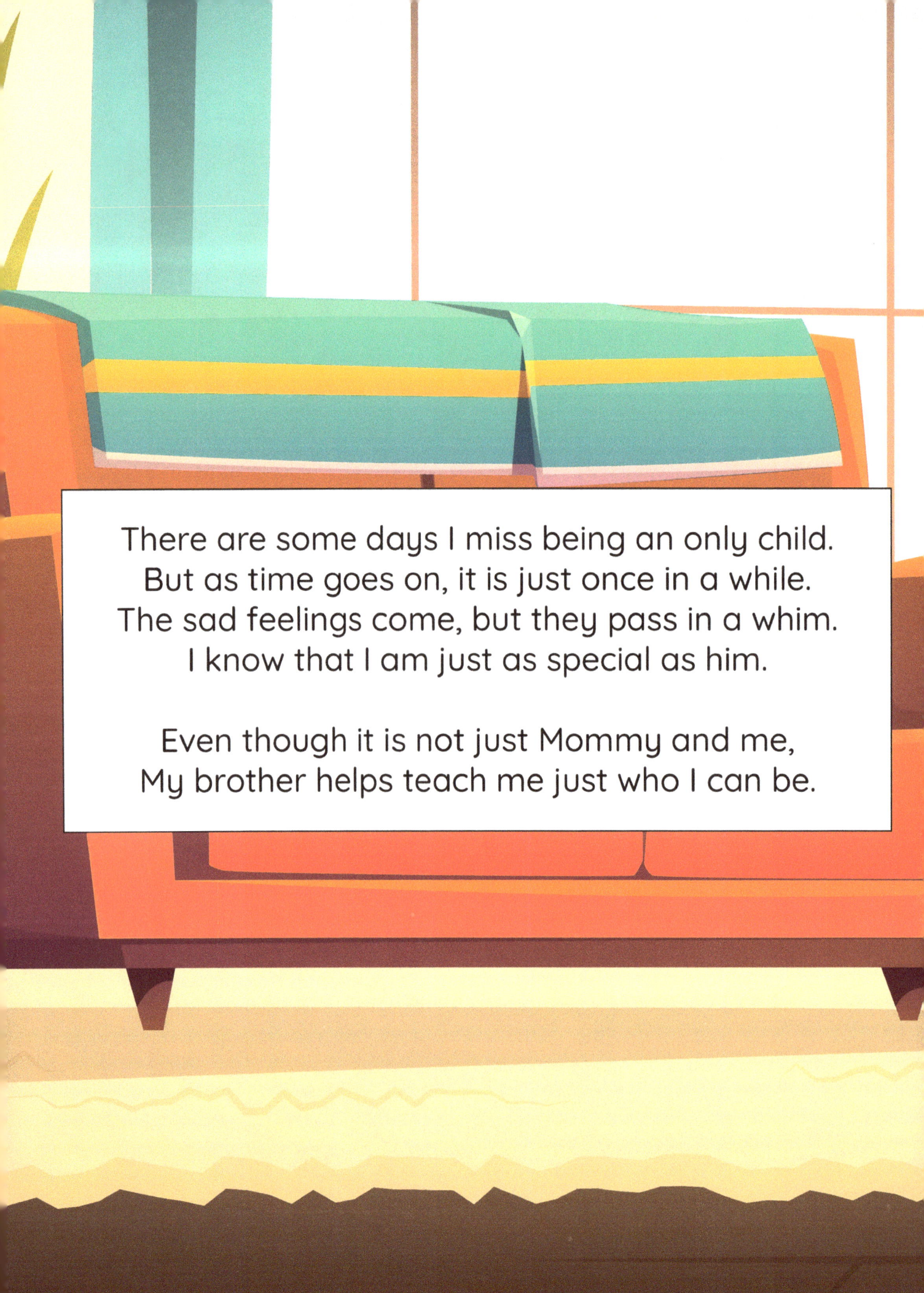

There are some days I miss being an only child.
But as time goes on, it is just once in a while.
The sad feelings come, but they pass in a whim.
I know that I am just as special as him.

Even though it is not just Mommy and me,
My brother helps teach me just who I can be.

He is Mom's baby. I am Mom's baby, too!
And there are some things only I get to do.

I have learned to be very patient
and help him, you see.
He tries his very best, but he is
not as healthy as me.

Although he needs some more attention at times,
I would never trade this family of mine!
Mommy was right – he's my best friend forever.
We have one another to love and treasure.

His challenges are a part of who he is.
But there is much more to that big heart of his!
He has disabilities, and I do not.
But I am just as special. How much? A lot!

www.ingramcontent.com/pod-product-compliance
Lightning Source LLC
Chambersburg PA
CBHW051305110526
44589CB00025B/2947